MY FIRST BOOK
ARGENTINA

ALL ABOUT ARGENTINA FOR KIDS

GLOBED
CHILDREN BOOKS

Interior and cover Design: Daniel Day
Editor: Margaret Bam

For My Sons, Daniel, David and Jude

Obelisco, Buenos Aires, Argentina

Argentina

Argentina is a country.

A country is land that is controlled by a single government. Countries are also called nations, states, or nation-states.

Countries can be different sizes. Some countries are big and others are small.

Valle del Cafayate, provincia de Salta, Argentina

Where Is Argentina?

Argentina is located in the continent of South America.

A continent is a massive area of land that is separated from others by water or other natural features.

Argentina is situated in the southern part of South America.

Panorama of the city of Buenos Aires

Capital

The capital of Argentina is Buenos Aires.

Buenos Aires is located in the eastern part of the country.

Buenos Aires is the largest city in Argentina.

San Telmo, Buenos Aires, Argentina

Provinces

Argentina is a country that is made up of 23 provinces

The provinces of Argentina are as follows:

Buenos Aires, Catamarca, Chaco, Chubut, Ciudad de Buenos Aires, Córdoba, Corrientes, Entre Ríos, Formosa, Jujuy, La Pampa, La Rioja, Mendoza, Misiones, Neuquén, Río Negro, Salta, San Juan, San Luis and Santa Cruz.

Bariloche, Argentina

Population

Argentina has population of around **47 million people** making it the 32nd most populated country in the world and the third most populated country in South America.

The people of Argentina are known for their rich cultural heritage, vibrant traditions, and deep passion for various forms of art and sports.

Iguazu Falls, Argentina

Size

Argentina is **2,780,400 square kilometres** making it the second largest country in South America by area.

Argentina is the 8th largest country in the world. The largest city in Argentina by area is Buenos Aires.

Languages

The official language of Argentina is Spanish. The Spanish language is now spoken by hundreds of millions of people across the world.

Here are a few Spanish phrases

- **Bienvenido** - Welcome
- **¿Cómo te llamas?** - What is your name?
- **¿Cómo estás?** - How are you?
- **Mucho gusto** - Nice to meet you
- **De nada** - You're welcome

Cabildo and Cordoba Cathedral, Cordoba, Argentina

Attractions

There are lots of interesting places to see in Argentina.

Some beautiful places to visit in Argentina are

- Iguazu Falls
- Teatro Colón
- Tierra del Fuego National Park
- Perito Moreno Glacier
- Recoleta Cemetery
- Mendoza

Beagle Channel, Ushuaia, Argentina

History of Argentina

People have lived in Argentina for a very long time, in fact there is evidence of human life in Argentina as far back as The Paleolithic period.

Europeans first arrived in the region with the 1502 voyage of Amerigo Vespucci.

Argentina gained independence from Spain on 9th July 1816.

Puerto Madero, Buenos Aires

Customs in Argentina

Argentina has many fascinating customs and traditions.

- Yerba Mate is the most popular drink in Argentina and it is customary to share it with your friend. Considered to be a social drink, many Argentines gather in parks passing around their drink.

- Football is exceptionally popular in Argentina. Argentines are passionate about their teams and players, and it is common for people to gather together watching the sport while chanting and playing music.

Music of Argentina

There are many different music genres in Argentina such as Tango music, Chacarera, Argentine rock, Argentine tango, Cumbia, Nueva canción, Cuarteto, Chamamé and Zamba.

Some notable Argentine musicians include
- León Gieco
- Gustavo Cerati
- Luis Alberto Spinetta
- Lali Espósito
- Diego Torres
- Andrés Calamaro
- Mercedes Sosa

Food of Argentina

Argentina is known for having delicious, flavoursome and rich dishes. The national dish of Argentina is asados which is a variety of barbecued meat grilled on a parillo.

Some popular dishes in Argentina include

- Asado
- Chimichurri
- Provoleta
- Empanadas
- Humita en chala

Mendoza, Argentina

Weather in Argentina

Argentina is a large country with a varied climate. The northern parts have a subtropical climate characterised by great heat and extensive rainfall, while the southern parts have a sub-Antarctic climate and can experience very cold weather.

Salta Argentina

Animals of Argentina

There are many wonderful animals in Argentina.

Here are some animals that live in Argentina

- Opossums
- Armadillos
- Rodents
- Bats
- Deers
- Capybaras
- Tapirs

Mar del Plata, Buenos Aires, Argentina

Beaches

There are many beautiful beaches in Argentina which is one of the reasons why so many people visit this beautiful country every year.

Here are some of Argentina's beaches

- Playa Bristol
- Puerto Madryn
- Villa Gesell
- Mar De Ajo
- Mar Del Plata
- Monte Hermoso

Fans supporting Argentina

Sports of Argentina

Sports play an integral part in Argentinian culture. The most popular sport is Football.

Here are some of famous sportspeople from Argentina

- Lionel Messi - Football
- Manu Ginóbili - Basketball
- Sergio Agüero - Football
- Ángel Di María - Football
- Alfredo Di Stéfano - Football

Bernardino Rivadavia

Notable Figures

Many successful people hail from Argentina.

Here are some notable Argentinian figures

- **Martina Stoessel – Singer**
- **Luisana Lopilato – Actress**
- **Juan Román Riquelme – Footballer**
- **Olivia Hussey – Actress**
- **Nicolás Otamendi – Footballer**
- **Eva Perón - Politician**
- **Bernardino Rivadavia - President**

La Boca, Argentina

Something Extra...

As a little something extra, we are going to share some lesser known facts about Argentina.

- The world's first animated feature film in 1917 was produced in Argentina.
- Argentina is home to both the highest and lowest points of the Southern Hemisphere.
- Argentina is the birthplace of tango.

Words From the Author

We hope that you enjoyed learning about the wonderful country of Argentina.

Argentina is a country rich in culture and beauty, with lots of wonderful places to visit and people to meet.

We hope you continue to learn more about this wonderful nation. If you enjoyed this book, consider leaving a review!

With Love

Made in the USA
Columbia, SC
17 December 2024

49820874R00024